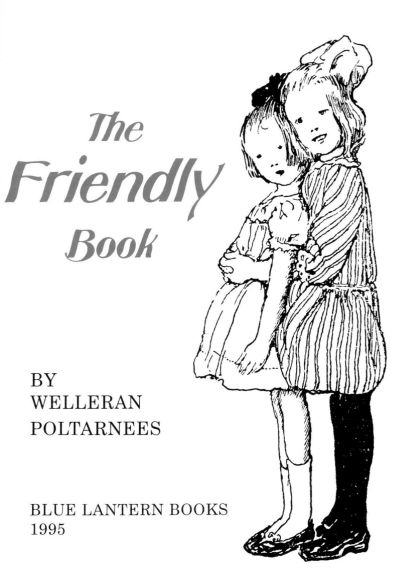

The Friendly Book

BY
WELLERAN
POLTARNEES

BLUE LANTERN BOOKS
1995

Second printing. Printed in Hong Kong.
ISBN 1-883211-05-0

Blue Lantern Books
PO Box 4399 • Seattle •Washington
98104-0399

Preface

Most of us are not grateful enough for the good things in our lives. We are blind to some of them because they are too familiar. The new bicycle or car is exciting. A vacation is a special pleasure. A gift, a holiday, a party, new clothes all thrill us in anticipation, and delight us in their coming. They are either expensive or demand planning, and are made to seem the high points of our lives because they are made so important.

We must continually remind ourselves that some of the best things are not expensive, or remarkable in their arrival, nor do they need to be elaborately planned for.

Friendship is one of these quiet gifts. We seldom go looking for it. We never have to pay. It arrives unexpectedly, often in unlikely places, but it is one of life's richest treasures.

W. P.

Life is to be fortified by many friendships.
To love and to be loved is the greatest
happiness of existence.

– Sydney Smith

**Friendship is for everyone. It is one
of the great joys of life, and makes all who
share it a little happier.**

There is no such thing as too many friends, just as there is never too much happiness.

– Jean de La Bruyère

Friendship is not just for two, many can join, and each is richer for the others.

Friendship is the unspeakable joy and blessing that result to two or more individuals who from constitution sympathize. Such natures are liable to no mistakes, but will know each other through thick and thin. Between two by nature alike, and fitted to sympathize, there is no veil, and there can be no obstacle. Who are the estranged? Two friends explaining.

– Henry David Thoreau

Between friends, words are unnecessary.

The very society of joy redoubles it; so that while it lights upon my friend it rebounds upon myself, and the brighter his candle burns the more easily it will light mine.
                                        – Robert South

We all enjoy activities more when we have found a friend with whom to share them with.

Of all the gifts that a wise providence grants us to make life full and happy, friendship is the most beautiful.

– Epicurus

The sharing of secrets, and the keeping of them, are two of the privileges of friendship.

I delight in nothing unless I have a friend to share it with.

– Seneca

We are more aware of the beauty of the world when a friend sees it with us.

The only rose without thorns is friendship.
– Horatio Scudder

Friendship makes happiness as fire makes heat.

Love is the cement that binds families together, but it is friendship that makes them happy.

— William Hazlitt

   Friendship is found within the family as well as without. Mothers, fathers, sisters, brothers – all of them can be the best of friends.

*Animals are such agreeable friends – they
ask you no questions. They pass no criticisms.*
– George Eliot

**Old friends are the best friends.
They understand us.**

If a man does not make new friends as he passes through life, he may find himself alone.

– Samuel Johnson

We are made new by our new friends.

Picture Credits

Front Cover
- Cecil Aldin. *The Merry Puppy Book*. 1913.

Endpapers (front)
- Maginel Wright Barney. Magazine illustration. 1926.

Frontispiece
- Harriett M. Bennett. *Queen of the Meadow*. *circa* 1891.

Title Page
- Sarah S. Stilwell. *Rhymes & Jingles*. 1904.

Copyright Page
- May Gibbs. *Scotty in Gumnut Land*. circa 1920.

Preface Page
- Ford, H.J. *Irish Fairy and Folk Tales*. Circa 1890.

Interior Pages
- Wilhelm Busch. *Lustige Bilder-Geschichten für Kinder*. circa 1900.
- Mrs. Ernest Ames. *Tim and The Dusty Man*. circa 1900.
- Olga Heese. Magazine illustration. 1939.
- Millicent Sowerby. *The Gay Book*. 1915.
- Florence K. Upton. *The Adventures of Borbee and the Wisp*. 1908.
- Anne Anderson. *The Little Busy Bee Book*. circa 1917.
- Norman Price. "Winter Fun." circa 1910.
- Cecil Aldin. *Cecil Aldin's Merry Party*. 1913.
- M.Boutet de Monvel. *Quand J'étais Petit*. 1886.
- Jessie Willcox Smith. Magazine illustration. 1917.
- Anonymous. Book illustration. circa 1880.
- Harry Anderson. Magazine illustration. 1949.
- Rose O'Neill. Magazine illustration. 1910.
- Anonymous. Book illustration. circa 1890.
- Honor C. Appleton. *The Bower Book*. 1922.
- Carl Larsson. *Ett Hem åt Solisdan*. 1895.
- Keith Henderson. *Green Mansions*. 1926.
- John R. Neill. *The Tin Woodman of Oz*. 1918.
- Robert L. Dickey. *Mr. & Mrs. Beans*. 1928.
- Gertrude M. Kay. *The Field-Martin Primer*. 1925.
- Uldene Trippe. *Tippytoes Comes to Town*. 1926.

Endpapers (back)
- M. Krestjanoff. *Martin et Tommy installés*. 1920.

Back Cover
- H.J Ford. *Irish Fairy Tales*. circa 1910.